OH MY GOD!
FAITH IN FATE

Haresh Sippy

BLUEROSE PUBLISHERS
India | U.K.

Copyright © Haresh Sippy 2023

All rights reserved by author. No part of this publication may be reproduced, stored in a retrieval system or transmitted in any form or by any means, electronic, mechanical, photocopying, recording or otherwise, without the prior permission of the author. Although every precaution has been taken to verify the accuracy of the information contained herein, the publisher assumes no responsibility for any errors or omissions. No liability is assumed for damages that may result from the use of information contained within.

BlueRose Publishers takes no responsibility for any damages, losses, or liabilities that may arise from the use or misuse of the information, products, or services provided in this publication.

For permissions requests or inquiries regarding this publication, please contact:

BLUEROSE PUBLISHERS
www.BlueRoseONE.com
info@bluerosepublishers.com
+91 8882 898 898
+4407342408967

ISBN: 978-93-5819-321-3

Cover design: Tushar More
Typesetting: Pooja Sharma

First Edition: October 2023

About the Author

Founder and CMD of Tema India Ltd., one of India's largest shell-and-tube heat exchanger manufacturers, Haresh Sippy is a multi-patent holder for the screw-plug technology used in refining clean fuels worldwide.

He describes writing as a passion. The thoughts flow from the challenges he faces from time to time. Empowering youth through vocational training is a step in this direction and a path to self-fulfilment. A pioneer in the field of process equipment manufacturing, Sippy has been working towards making India self-reliant for nearly five decades.

Contents

Introduction 1
1. My Mother 5
2. Enlightenment Through Self-Discovery 9
3. Exploring the Depths of Meditation 11
4. God has Nothing to Give 13
5. Embracing Divine Guidance: The Voice of the Commoners 16
6. God Resides Within 21
7. Poems on God 30
8. Reflections on Life 66

Introduction

First things first. Drawing from the title of the book, *faith in fate* is a concept that may initially seem contradictory but essentially refers to having faith in oneself. It acknowledges that our lives are influenced by circumstances beyond our control, such as those we are born into. However, what we make of them is within our power. By having faith in our abilities and ourselves, we align with a higher power or purpose, often referred to as God.

In the pages of this book, I invite you to join me on a soul-stirring exploration that bridges the gap between our earthly endeavours and the unseen forces that shape our lives. We explore the vast mosaic of human experience, uncovering the whispers of the divine in ordinary moments, and revealing how God's presence is not confined to temples or shrines, but instead permeates every aspect of existence.

With reverence and open hearts, we embark on a transformative journey that celebrates the interconnectedness of all beings and emphasizes the universal truth that God resides within us, in fleeting moments of serendipity, and within the intricate webs of destiny that guide our lives.

Through profound insights, inspiring anecdotes and powerful revelations, this book promises to challenge your preconceptions, spark thought-provoking contemplation, and ignite within you a renewed sense of awe for the wondrous bonds between faith and fate. This statement acknowledges the incredible capabilities that exist within every individual, as well as the never-ending influence of divine guidance throughout our journey on Earth.

So, embrace these pages with an open mind and an ardent heart, for together, we shall unravel the mysteries of faith in fate and deepen our understanding of the awe-inspiring presence of God that permeates every corner of our existence.

Welcome to the journey, where faith intertwines with fate, and the divine unfolds before our very eyes.

When our hearts tremble with doubt, faith in fate reminds us that everything happens for a reason.

Like a symphony of destinies, faith illuminates the harmony hidden within the fabric of fate.

Embrace the twists and turns with unwavering faith, for fate's design is more beautiful than we can imagine.

In the tapestry of life, faith weaves the threads of our dreams into the extraordinary pattern of fate.

With faith in fate, we surrender our fears and allow life's unpredictable winds to carry us towards our destiny.

When the stars align and opportunities arise, faith in fate becomes the propeller that propels us towards greatness.

By truly believing in our path, we discover our purpose, for faith in fate shapes our journey into a masterpiece.

To Surrender is to place #FaithInFate's Hand

To surrender is to release our grip on control,
Embracing the unknown, letting destiny unfold.
With faith as our compass, guiding the way,
Trusting in Fate's wisdom, come what may.

It is not an act of weakness, but of strength untold,
A surrender that nurtures growth, as stories unfold.
For in surrendering, we find a tranquil grace,
Embracing the ebb and flow of life's relentless pace.

#FaithInFate illuminates our path divine,
Guiding us closer to victories that intertwine.
With surrender, we entrust our dreams and desire,
Allowing the essence of destiny to transpire.

In surrender, we yield to the lessons to be learned,
Knowing that every twist and turn has its turn.
With faith as our ally, we navigate the unknown,
As Fate weaves together a tapestry uniquely our own.

So let us surrender, with hopeful hearts aglow,
Trusting in the unfolding of life's grand tableau.
In the dance with Fate, we find courage and grace,
Embracing the changes and finding our rightful place.

#FaithInFate, an unwavering embrace,
Reminding us that surrendering holds no disgrace.
For in letting go, we discover life's truest beat,
And find solace in the paths Fate will complete.

1. My Mother

My mom passed away on May 30th, 2023, a few months before her 98th birthday. Though it may seem illogical, my beliefs are rooted beyond everyday reasoning, and governed by faith in fate. I took the decision to engage in all of the rituals with my son, no matter how unique or exhausting they were. This allowed me to feel a sense of unity as I shared these responsibilities with my only son, and assured me that even though my mom's body is lifeless, her soul rests content. Her only desire was for us to be united, as she was concerned about my late father and me, and now my son and I can continue on as one.

I wasn't concerned with superficial traditions being upheld for the sake of impressing outsiders. Rather, I felt a connection between the souls of my deceased mother and my son together for a cause that is essential to successfully running the newly acquired family business. We were fully committed to each and every rite. I feel that these rituals are important in all religions because they teach discipline, which is especially important for people who lack it. For instance, while fasting may not be necessary for individuals with consistent eating habits, it's essential for the obese whose gluttonous tendencies perpetuate their unhealthy weight. Similarly, a dedicated worker is already disciplined, but a person who is kamchor (lazy) should follow the complete set of rituals.

I had ongoing discussions with Panditji that lasted until the funeral rites. He advised me to do what was morally just, but it troubled me, as it seemed to involve ethics. Whereas morals and ethics are about what's right and what's wrong. Morals are usually shaped by a person's personal beliefs and values while ethics are more formalized and agreed upon by society to regulate behavior in groups or professions. In short, morals are spiritual and subjective whereas ethics are objective and worldly

The rituals were to continue for twelve days and the things to do and not to do were possible only if Akhil (my son) and I took a Sannyasa for these days. We did not participate in all the rituals but continued to focus on everyday work obligations. My son and I both had an innate sense of what needed to be done, without even discussing or consciously thinking about it. By working diligently, we aimed to lead by example and convey the message to our employees that "work is worship," and every task is an opportunity for reverence and dedication.

We firmly believe that all activities, no matter how small, should be given the same level of thoughtful attention and focus that rituals command, to cultivate gratitude and an integrated sense of being, which not only enables us to prioritize and manage our roles effectively but also enhances the quality of life.

We were immersed in work, adhering to the principle of "work is worship," which my mother instilled in me from childhood. Although certain rituals, like feeding a cow every day, were followed, some were not. As my mom would have wanted, we dedicated ourselves to our work. I just concluded rightly or wrongly that every activity we engage in, for the good of everyone is a ritual to be performed

As I reminisce about the moments shared with my mom during our younger years, it has dawned on me that we tend to overlook the importance of our loved ones, just as we often do with God. We may undervalue their love and support and make the mistake of not cherishing what they have given us, eventually losing out on all that they have to give. The path ahead is to dwell upon the love that we receive and give compassionately, knowing the greater good that comes from gratitude and appreciation.

My mother, despite not having a high level of education, had a practical and resourceful mindset. She was a refugee from Sindh and faced many challenging situations, but she always maintained her dignity. Observing how she dealt with difficult circumstances with poise and effectiveness was a valuable learning experience for me.

My mother's talents also extended to the arts of cooking and stitching, and I was fortunate to have imbibed her expertise in these areas. To this day, I value her teachings and cherish memories of the many meals and designs that she shared with us.

Religions are man-made institutions based on a set of beliefs, practices, traditions, and values that have evolved over time through different interpretations, cultural contexts and experiences, and social interactions. However, they share a number of commonalities, particularly when it comes to the values of principles of humanity and spirituality. Numerous religions assert their commitment to promoting humanity, mutual respect, and tolerance towards other religions and cultures. However, interpretational differences can indeed lead to misunderstanding and misconceptions about the essence of religion. Some interpretations could be inspired by biases, personal opinions, or cultural norms, and even radical ideas affecting human rights.

As a result, the way various religious beliefs get operationalized might not always reflect their core ethics and values, leading to potential conflicts with humanity. Societies need to encourage dialogue and interfaith programs that promote mutual understanding, respect, and tolerance. This will help us all live in peace and harmony, which is the true meaning behind all religions. You may not believe, but not respecting someone else's beliefs is really immoral.

I feel compelled to express my thoughts through quotes and poetry, depending on how much space I need to fully convey my message.

2. Enlightenment Through Self-Discovery

Mythology often refers to ancient texts that contain timeless wisdom for humankind. These texts span generations, perhaps even centuries, and are shrouded in mystery about their true origins. To fully comprehend the information, one must embark on a voyage of self-discovery and reflection. This knowledge can be so profound that the seeker may feel compelled to share it with others. However, when it comes to how this knowledge is shared, the method is just as important as the message.

Using tales and stories is often a more engaging and memorable method of sharing knowledge with a larger audience. Over time, such stories can become foundational in religion and guide the beliefs and practices of people of faith. One challenge is that when people become too rigid in their beliefs, they can start enforcing them instead of simply following them.

When this happens, religion can often become a set of rules created by those in positions of unquestioned authority. In doing so, followers can lose sight of the true essence of the wisdom contained in the ancient texts. By focusing on rituals and gestures in the hopes of influencing God, rather than embodying the overarching principles of that wisdom.

Throughout the ages, inflexible and close-minded religious convictions have frequently led to discrimination, subjugation, and even conflicts fought in the name of religious piety. It is essential that we remind ourselves that the essence of these ancient texts is not about us finding God; instead, it's about discovering if we are with God or not.

It's a problem when we fear God as this fear is often the result of us losing sight of our true divine nature. We are conditioned to fight so fiercely for our religious views that we forget that only a small effort is all we need for self-improvement rather than destruction. The Creator, God, does not belong exclusively to any specific religious group or sect. rather, it is nectar that removes the petty discrimination and divisions between people.

True disciples of God are individuals who become fit both inside and outside. Self-improvement starts with self-acceptance and love. Recognize the good in others and focus on personal growth. By absorbing the sacred texts and ingesting their true essence within ourselves, and through self-reflection and introspection, we can acquire true self-realization. The result will be a seeing of God within ourselves and in every human being around us.

Humanity is the crux of true spirituality. It's about recognizing that every human being is unique and precious and that we should view each other with respect, kindness, and love. We can achieve this by humanising the essence of the ancient practices of these profound books, thus achieving peaceful coexistence. Such a principle is what all religions aspire to achieve and stands as an embodiment of universal love and human togetherness.

3. Exploring the Depths of Meditation

Meditation—an ancient practice that has stood the test of time—is often seen as the harmonious blending of the free and controlled mind. In this article, we delve into the multifaceted nature of meditation, guided by both traditional wisdom and contemporary insights. Our goal is to explore the benefits of meditation and how it can positively impact our lives by sharing our perspectives and ideas.

The Body-Mind Connection in Meditation

At the core of meditation lies the connection between the body and the mind. Through practices such as yoga, deep breathing, and mindful movement, we cultivate awareness and presence in the present moment. By syncing our breath with our movements, we invite oxygen to fuel our bodies and engage our minds, inviting a sense of balance and centeredness.

Disciplining the Mind

One of the fundamental aspects of meditation is the art of disciplining the mind. When we purposely concentrate our thoughts, we can separate ourselves from negative influences and disruptions. This allows us to establish a productive environment for gaining clarity and understanding. It is through this intentional focus that we can enhance our concentration, making us more efficient in both work and play.

Beyond Traditional Boundaries

Although meditation has long been associated with sitting quietly in one place, it has a much broader scope. The beauty of meditation lies in its versatility—it can be integrated into every aspect of our lives. Whether we are savoring a meal, playing a lively game, or caught up in a heated argument, meditation helps us discover a sense of calmness and steadiness amidst the commotion.

Living on the Edge

Let us consider meditation as living on the edge—with the thrill of pushing limits and embracing life's challenges while maintaining a state of calm. Our true potential and innate wisdom are unlocked by maintaining a delicate balance. By living beyond the confines of societal rules, we empower ourselves to fully experience life, all while staying in control.

Through the journey of this article, we have come to appreciate the true essence of meditation—a practice that beautifully blends the body and mind guides us in living fully and allows us to stabilize and harness the power of our thoughts and emotions. As we delve deeper into the practice of meditation and incorporate it into our lives, it's important to keep in mind that it's a journey that lasts a lifetime. It requires finding a balance between relinquishing control and maintaining discipline, and offers limitless opportunities for personal growth and change.

When we have a brilliant idea, we spend time showing it instead of being wise to get a lot more thoughts to back it up.

It can be tempting to share or take action on a brilliant idea as soon as it comes to mind. However, taking the time to reflect and gather more thoughts to back up our idea can be incredibly valuable. By giving ourselves space for further contemplation and exploration, we allow for the possibility of improving and refining our initial idea. By seeking wisdom and considering multiple perspectives, we can develop more comprehensive and nuanced concepts. While it may be tempting to share our ideas immediately, taking the time to gather more thoughts and insights can lead to even greater success and fulfillment.

4. God has Nothing to Give

"God has given us more than we desire, yet we often fail to realize,

His blessings are abundant, a treasure before our eyes.

In gratitude, let us recognize the gifts we receive,

For in the depths of His love, we can truly believe."

God has bestowed upon us various powers, and it is important that we learn to utilize them instead of becoming consumed by a hunger for power.

Realizing and appreciating the potential within ourselves is important. It is indeed essential to learn how to harness our abilities in order to create positive change and fulfillment in our lives, rather than seeking power for its own sake. It's an excellent reminder to focus on using our abilities and talents for the greater good and the benefit of ourselves and others.

Be a Rishi

Oh, mundane thoughts, how they weigh us down,
But a free soul, a true jewel to be found,
In this journey of life, we seek to be free,
Living boundless, like the vast sea.
A free soul, a free mind, soaring high,
Thoughts aligned, reaching for the sky,
Breaking free from the chains that bind,
Embracing freedom, leaving worries behind.

A burdened soul, held tight by its fears,
Imprisoned within, it sheds no tears,
But a free soul, it persists in peace,
A rishi's spirit, let it never cease.

In this symphony, let us all unite,
With love and freedom, we will ignite,
A harmonious journey, boundless and clear,
Oh, may our souls be forever sincere.

So let us break the chains that hold us tight,
Radiate love, in all shades so bright,
A free soul, a free mind, let it be,
Our anthem of liberation, forever set free

Entrepreneurship encompasses the pursuit of aspirations driven by personal passions, rather than being solely fixated on achieving specific ambitions.

Entrepreneurship is driven by passions rather than being obsessed with achieving certain ambitions can lead to a more fulfilling and purpose-driven entrepreneurial journey. When our enthusiasm for our work and the influence we aim to generate is strong, we are inclined to maintain motivation, resilience, and unwavering commitment to realizing our concepts. It allows an entrepreneur to focus on what truly matters and make a positive difference in their chosen field.

Passion vs Ambition:

I'd rather be ambitious about my passions,
Than be passionate about my ambitions.
In the fire's embrace, fulfilment yearns,
Passions guide me as my world brightly turns.

In the depths of my soul, I find endless desire,
A flame that ignites, setting my dreams on fire.
For it is in pursuing what truly brings me joy,
That I unlock the power within to truly employ.

With each step forward, ambition lights the way,
A driving force that keeps distractions at bay.
For it is not in mere ambition for its own sake,
But in following my passions, I find what it takes.

So, I'll remain steadfast, embracing my true path,
Letting my passions guide me, protecting from wrath.
For a life filled with purpose and heartfelt zeal,
Is worth more than any ambition alone could seal.

5. Embracing Divine Guidance: The Voice of the Commoners

When God communicates with us, His word is often conveyed through the voice of ordinary people.

One movie that comes to mind is *Darkest Hour*, which I saw at Inox cinema, Nariman Point before Covid set in. Generally, I do not have the patience to sit in the theatre for too long, but in this case, I was glued to the screen because there was so much to absorb. I would like to mention the impactful parts.

Winston Churchill's conversation with a child is a touching example of trusting divine direction in the face of hardship. The enlightenment seen on Churchill's face said it all. There are various ways in which spiritual direction might reveal itself, often via the unassuming voices of ordinary people. Recognising that God's teachings reach us via all people teaches us the importance of accepting the knowledge hidden in their life experiences, viewpoint and insights. This awakening to divine wisdom opens the door to a more profound understanding and connection with the divine.

Taking inspiration from Winston Churchill's travels during World War II, let us examine his decision to take a tube ride to connect with ordinary people in the middle of political turbulence and the transformational character of this uncommon act.

Churchill's conversations with a varied spectrum of people throughout his tube journey are presented. These conversations capture both, their brief encounters and the influence their remarks had on the Prime Minister's perspective. The conversations bring forth the feelings, anxieties and hopes voiced by the commoners, delivering a clear depiction of their effect on Churchill's state of mind. This marks a watershed moment in the Prime Minister's journey. As their voices blend, a child freely expresses her opinions to Churchill and provides him with profoundly-felt advice. In her steadfast belief, she utters words that reverberate in his mind: *You can do it. You can do it.*

Exploring the significant influence of the discussion with the little girl, consider the long-term significance of accepting heavenly counsel communicated by ordinary people. The conversation between Churchill and the youngster is a stunning reminder of the impact that ordinary voices may have in changing history and inspiring change. Churchill was transformed by this contact with heavenly insight, motivating him to give his memorable speeches and lead Britain through its darkest hour.

Poem

In the darkest hour, wisdom gleams,
As God's whisper echoes in our dreams.
Through common souls, His voice reveals,
The power within to forge ideal ideals.

From Churchill's tale, we learn with grace,
Choice resounds in life's challenging race.
In the little girl's words, innocence unfurled,
Guidance from above, for a better world.

Communal wisdom, a beacon's light,
Amidst the chaos, shining bright.
Within each voice, a fragment of truth,
Listen closely, awaken the sleuth.

Social standing holds no sway,
In this quest for wisdom, each has a say.
Blend perspectives, opinions combine,
Wisdom's tapestry formed a design so fine.

Let us embrace this philosophy rare,
Harness our power, willing to dare.
Through choices made, with discernment keen,
We shape our lives, fulfilling the divine scheme.

1. God speaks to us through whispers, but often we drown His voice in the noise of our desires.
2. The power of divine guidance lies dormant within us, waiting patiently for us to awaken and listen.
3. In silence, God speaks. In the chaos, He waits. It is up to us to create the space to hear His voice.
4. We are never alone; God's presence surrounds us. We only need to turn inward and tune our hearts to His gentle whispers.
5. When we ignore the whispers of the divine, we deny ourselves the wisdom and love that could guide our lives towards greatness.

6. To seek God is to listen actively. His voice echoes through the winds and whispers through the hearts of those who know how to listen.

7. The noise of the world can make us deaf to the divine, but within us lies the power to clear the clutter and hear His voice with clarity.

8. When our hearts are open, our minds still, and our intentions pure, God's voice resonates within, leading us towards a path filled with purpose and peace.

9. We often seek God's guidance in grand gestures but fail to recognise that He speaks to us through the smallest of whispers and subtlest of signs.

10. The divine power speaks to us not only in moments of triumph and clarity but in the depths of our trials and confusion. His voice carries the wisdom we need to navigate life's challenges.

Poem

God speaks to us in the gentle rustle of leaves,
In the hushed whispers of ripples on the seas.
His voice is found in the songbirds' melody,
And in the symphony of stars above, so heavenly.

He speaks to our hearts when we are still,
Guiding us towards His purpose with an unyielding will.
In moments of joy, His voice sparks a gleam,
Reassuring us that in His love we will forever dream.

Yet, we often ignore His tender call,
Caught up in the clamour, letting distractions enthrall.
But if we quiet our minds, and open our ears,
God's voice becomes crystal clear, dispelling all fears.

Through whispers and signs, God shares His grace,
Guiding us with love in every uncertain place.
So, let us tune in, listen closely and be still,
For in the silence, God speaks, heart to heart, providing the thrill.

6. God Resides Within

"The deer persists, chasing the elusive scent of musk, knowing it lies within its own navel. Similarly, we seek God, residing within ourselves, tirelessly journeying in pursuit of divine connection."

Amidst the expanse of the wild, the elegant deer wanders and sprints ceaselessly, in search of the alluring fragrance of musk. It explores the terrain relentlessly, forever chasing that enchanting scent, oblivious to the fact that the very essence it desires resides within its own navel. Observing this pursuit is truly captivating, as the outcome reflects our own journey towards a greater truth.

In our human existence, we embark upon a lifelong search for meaning, purpose, and a connection with the divine. We traverse landscapes of experience, engaging in various beliefs and practices, seeking solace and fulfillment. However, it is within these fervent pursuits that we frequently miss the most profound verity: the celestial spark abides within each of us, patiently anticipating its revelation.

The metaphor of the deer's pursuit of musk reminds us that our own pursuit of God is ultimately an exploration of our innermost being. The realization that the divine resides within us brings new meaning to our quest, transforming it into an intimate journey of self-discovery and connection with the divine. In this sacred pursuit, may we find solace and fulfillment, and ultimately embrace the profound truth that we are divinely intertwined with the fabric of the universe.

In thickets deep where silence lies,
A deer roams beneath the skies.
In noble stride, it seeks to find,
The fragrant musk that lies entwined.

With eyes wide, the deer does quest,
For the very essence in its chest,
Yet unaware, it searches far,
For the musk is born just where they are.

A mirror to our own pursuit,
We seek a truth that lies in root,
In awe we marvel at this sight,
The deer's own journey, our own plight.

For deep within our souls do dwell,
The sacred secret we must unveil,
A spark divine, an inner flame,
God's presence there, one and the same.
Yet, oftentimes we roam astray,
In search of God in distant ways,
We overlook where truth is found,
In our own hearts, on sacred ground.

For God resides within us all,
Beyond dividing lines that sprawl,
In unity, we shall be blessed,
By knowing God within our chest.

So, let's embrace what deer imparts,
The wisdom held within their hearts,
That God's presence is our own,
In sacred stillness, we are known.

***

"What is subjective is not to be dismissed, for it is rooted in individual experiences and thus holds inherent value."

The concept of subjectivity is often misunderstood or undervalued in our society. Subjectivity refers to individual perspectives, opinions, and experiences that are unique to each person. While subjectivity is often contrasted with objectivity, it should not be underestimated or disregarded.

Individual subjectivity takes form through the intricate weaving of personal experiences, emotions, and perspectives, imbuing our comprehension of the world with a vivid array of hues. It acknowledges the inherent diversity of human existence and recognizes that each individual brings a distinct lens through which they interpret and interact with the world around them.

What makes subjectivity valuable is precisely its deeply personal nature. It enables people to apply their own perspectives, feelings, and backgrounds to any given scenario or issue. This diversity of perspectives can enrich our understanding and foster empathy, as we learn to appreciate different viewpoints and engage in meaningful dialogue.

Ultimately, subjectivity is valuable since it involves personal experiences, viewpoints, and emotions. Recognizing and valuing subjectivity may develop understanding, empathy, personal growth, and a more nuanced understanding of the human experience. We welcome the diversity and individuality that make our world dynamic and meaningful by embracing subjectivity.

> "The only way to truly live is in the present moment. However, by being time conscious, we often miss out because time is either in the past or the future. The present is a momentary joy that is timeless."

Indeed, when we fully immerse ourselves in the present moment, it has a transformative power to transcend the boundaries of time. In the realm of pure presence, time loses its grip and our experiences become timeless. It is in these precious moments of complete presence that we truly connect with the essence of life and embrace the infinite possibilities that unfold before us. So, let us embrace the present and make our every moment a timeless masterpiece.

> "Our intelligence is mostly influenced by external factors, which can give it an artificial appearance unless it is actively nurtured and developed."

Intelligence can indeed be influenced by external factors, such as education, upbringing, and exposure to various experiences and information. These influences can shape and enhance an individual's intellectual abilities. However, it's essential to note that intelligence is not solely determined by external factors. People have innate cognitive abilities that form the foundation of their intelligence. While external influences play a role in developing and maximizing intellectual potential, intelligence itself is not inherently artificial.

By actively engaging in learning, critical thinking, problem-solving, and acquiring knowledge, individuals can develop and expand their intelligence. So, while external influences undoubtedly play a part, intelligence is not solely enforced or artificial. It is a combination of innate capabilities and the opportunities and efforts taken to enhance and expand one's cognitive abilities.

> *"Why exclusively focus all your efforts on learning about external factors when AI can assist you, instead of pursuing the fulfillment of your desires?"*

It's a matter of personal choice and preference. While AI technology can assist with various tasks and provide convenience, the pursuit of personal growth and fulfillment extends beyond relying solely on external factors such as AI. Learning and self-improvement encompass the broadening of knowledge, the acquisition of fresh skills, the exploration of interests, and the nurturing of personal passions. These undertakings collectively foster intellectual, emotional, and spiritual advancement, culminating in overall well-being and self-satisfaction.

While AI has the potential to amplify specific facets of our existence, it might not encapsulate the entirety of human experiences, longings, and aspirations. The quest for fulfillment frequently entails a blend of internal introspection and the utilization of external resources, including AI, as aids to support our journey.

Ultimately, the decision on how to allocate efforts and time between learning external factors and working towards personal desires is a subjective choice that varies from person to person. It's important to find a balance that aligns with individual goals and values.

> "If doctors could prioritize teaching and guiding, rather than solely focusing on treatment,
>
> If engineers could prioritize designing methods to safeguard against carbon emissions, rather than prioritizing profit at the expense of causing pollution,
>
> If lawyers could emphasize preaching justice and integrity, instead of exploiting legal loopholes,
>
> If humanity sought spiritual enlightenment, instead of engaging in holy wars,
>
> The world would emerge as a heavenly realm, and life itself would embody paradise."

Expanding on the notion that doctors could prioritize teaching and guiding, we envision a healthcare system that not only diagnoses and treats illnesses but also educates individuals on preventive measures, healthy lifestyles, and self-care. Doctors would work as mentors, allowing patients to become active participants in their own health. This emphasis on education would result in a society that is better equipped to prioritize holistic health, leading to a decrease in chronic illnesses and an overall improvement in the quality of life.

Continuing with the notion that engineers may prioritize developing solutions to reduce carbon emissions, we envision a world where technology and innovation are driven by a strong commitment to environmental sustainability. Earth-friendly solutions would be at the forefront of every engineering project, ensuring that economic progress goes hand in hand with the preservation of our planet. This shift in focus would lead to the development and implementation of greener industries, renewable energy sources, and eco-friendly infrastructure, mitigating the harmful impacts of pollution and climate change.

In this transformed world, the collaboration of doctors, engineers, lawyers, and humanity as a whole would lead to a truly heavenly realm. Life would be marked by a profound feeling of peace in which people cohabit with nature, technology is ecologically mindful, justice reigns supreme, and spiritual enlightenment pervades all aspects of society. The vision of paradise would emerge via each individual's conscious decisions and acts, resulting in a world that is not only sustainable but also filled with love, peace, and a deep awareness for the interconnection of all creatures.

> *"The concept of solely focusing on one thing at a time is considered outdated, as any deviation serves as an opportunity for fresh thinking and exploration."*

In the past, the concept of multitasking was often seen as a skill or trait that individuals needed to develop in order to be efficient and productive. However, as our understanding of cognitive processes and neuroplasticity has evolved, we have come to realize that exclusive single-task focus may no longer be the most effective approach.

Moreover, the rapid pace of modern life demands our ability to quickly switch between tasks and adapt to changing circumstances. This flexibility and adaptability are essential in navigating today's complex and dynamic world. By embracing deviations and interruptions as opportunities for fresh thinking, we become more agile and responsive in our problem-solving and decision-making.

The notion of exclusively focusing on one thing at a time as the most efficient approach is being challenged. Allowing for deviations and new ideas may lead to enhanced creativity, flexibility, and innovation. By being open to diverse ideas and leveraging the power of our wandering minds, we can navigate the complexity of the modern world more effectively and make significant advancements in various fields.

> *"In the courageous journey of self-analysis, we confront the blocks that confine us, daring to dismantle them. Through the painful process, we find liberation, unlocking the path to authenticity and unleashing the power within."*

The blocks that dictate the dos and don'ts in life, creating limitations and constraints, require careful analysis and examination for liberation. This process can indeed be difficult and challenging, often accompanied by discomfort and pain. However, it is through this courageous exploration that we can unravel the layers of conditioning and self-imposed restrictions, ultimately freeing ourselves to live authentically and aligned with our true desires.

Confronting these impediments demands extensive introspection and self-reflection. We must be willing to challenge society conventions, cultural expectations, and even deeply held beliefs and concerns. It may entail exploring previous traumas, unearthing buried emotions, and confronting the discomfort that comes with breaking long-held habits of thinking and behavior.

Finally, by analyzing and releasing the barriers that limit us, we uncover the possibility for development, emancipation, and full self-expression. While uncomfortable, confronting discomfort is a bold act that leads us to live a life that is honest, aligned, and in tune with our innermost wants and objectives.

Embrace the discomfort of self-analysis, for within its depths lies the key to release the blocks that bind you, paving the way to your true freedom.

In the crucible of self-reflection, we challenge the dos and don'ts that stifle our growth, igniting a transformation that sets our spirits free.

The path to liberation is marked by the willingness to face the painful truths that reside within, demolishing the barriers that hinder our true potential.

Break the chains of societal conditioning through the courageous exploration of self, for it is in the shadows of discomfort that we find the light of our authentic existence.

7. Poems on God

My God!

It is not the religion, but we who are the God's creation.
How do we get one God but so many religions?

Who then do we worship? May I ask in all humility?
The answer lies in the question, why not humanity?

We say God is omnipresent and so He is present in all of us
Why then we don't love God within and in all the others?

God has given us everything to live and let live, there's nothing to be sought.
He wants us to enjoy without hesitation, so let's stop putting words in His mouth.

Love is God

Why limit your love to a person when God in each one of us resides?
Love is God is the credo by which every creed abides.

Love is not between people; it reaches out to the purity within;
It appeals to the nobility of the heart, the simplicity within.

We maybe outwardly attracted to the one beside us
But true love connects with the goodness inside us.

What a miracle the Almighty performs for me
I now see my beloved in every face I see…

Not What You Think

*Don't do what you think God has decreed,
What you want is the will of God indeed;*

*The heavens granted, long before you knew,
The Giver doesn't expect anything from you;*

*His benefaction lies unappreciated and ignored,
Greed compels you to accumulate and hoard;*

*What is invaluable cannot be cumulated,
Joy comes from within, it can never be created;*

*Wellbeing is not something you obtain on a platter,
A healthy mind in a healthy body must matter;*

*Life is a joy, but we are told to think otherwise,
In attachment we forsake the freedom of the skies.*

Inward Journey

Beauty is all around us, not appreciating it is a sin,
How will we ever see it, if we do not look within?

The beauty we all look for is only on the surface,
Real beauty is within the truth, which we must trace;

Why are we concerned with what others perceive?
Why pretend what we are not, and ourselves deceive

Have faith in fate and surrender to God who resides within
Let the positive energy flow, and the inward journey begin

What God Wants

Don't do what God wants,
What you want is what God wants,

Neither has He anything for you,
Nor does he want anything from you,

He has already given you everything,
But you have not accepted anything,

All His gifts for you are lying in the bin,
The devil in you says the gifts are sin,

Building your identity is all fake,
Do everything for your health's sake,

Your character is not what you obtain,
The health of mind and body you must maintain,
Life is a joy but we are told to think otherwise,
Attachments are holy, we're compelled to think likewise,

When shouldering all blames become recreation,
It's the ultimate destination and you enjoy salvation.

Thanksgiving

God provides what you deserve, not what you desire,
What you deserve is not the same as what you acquire;

Accept this and you will enjoy His benevolence,
With His creation, you will be in resonance;

Acceptance is a process that happens in the fullness of time,
A path of evolution, which must be our concern prime;

Doing what God wants is fulfilling and empowering,
It is the salvation for which we must offer thanksgiving.

Lord and Master

Lord Shiva has three eyes the third one with a vision
The right looks at positivity and the left for a reason

The third eye is the one that balances the two.
The one that is more direct than the other two

The other two look at an angle and report to either side of the brain.
Shiva's third eye controls the right eye the left without any constrain.

The right side is purposeless whereas the left is full of purpose
One is the positive energy and the other is absolutely righteous

One is pure divinity, the other the applied discipline
They are two-in-one like the ego and the alter ego within

Positivity is synonymous with Energy, this is what Lord Shiva provides
Bajrangbali, a symbol of strength, who motivates and guides

One is the lord of morals, the other, the master of ethics
The combination of the lord and the master is moral-ethics

Basic Instinct

One should rather be a selfish person than live in the fear of being called one,
Selflessness comes from loving oneself, thereby loving everyone;

We don't love ourselves for the fear of being called selfish,
God is omnipresent, He's in all of us, and we bow to His wish;

Selfishness comes from the basic instinct of survival,
Selflessness comes from faith in fate, the power of revival;

If only everyone was selfish and no one pretended to be otherwise,
This truth is universal understanding, with nothing in disguise;

There would be no false claims and no justification desired,
No differences, no disputes, no clarifications required;
We will then start loving ourselves and each other,
Thereby, loving the God inside us and in one another.

Blessings from Within

Why do we go out to seek His blessings all the time?
His blessings are our very existence, but not worth a dime,

Should He be partial and bless one more than the other?
Is worship drawing His attention, competing with one another?

Every human on this planet is seeking His favour,
We fight tooth and nail, and make every endeavour;

What if everyone's prayers were answered in affirmation?
Wouldn't there be chaos and much contradiction?

Is He going to discriminate or fulfil the demands of everyone?
What if one's blessing turns out to be a curse for someone?

Therefore, God does not bless you, His creation does, make this your belief,
God's blessings come from people when you make them smile in relief;

When the inner you make you help someone against your wishes,
That's salvation, you feel blessed from within and your soul flourishes.

Don't Lookout for God

Stop looking for God, He's been chasing you,
You're the one running away without a clue;

God is neither in an image, nor does He in a holy place reside,
He has always been within you, why don't you look inside?

Be good to everyone, as God resides in them all,
Talks to you through them, when He takes a call;

When God resides in you, it becomes a place of worship,
Keep it clean and healthy, and with positivity equip.

Enjoy for God's sake

When the work we do is what we love, do we need a break?
We don't have to do what we don't want to do, for God's sake;

Why do we need a break from work, don't we enjoy it?
A machine can do what we don't enjoy, let's deploy it;

When we take a break, do we enjoy or is it a compulsion?
To show off how much we enjoy becomes an obligation;

If we do not differentiate between work and play,
We are free to do what we like, it's a break all the way.

God Fearing

We are made to fear God for the godmen to thrive,
Let's not fear if we want the God within to survive;

All the wrongs are done in the name of the Lord,
Our freedom is taken away by the very men of the God;

Religion enforced by war is the cause of fear and bad blood,
The dos and don'ts that come along, must be nipped in the bud;

Unfortunately, in the name of religion we cause a divide,
Humanity is the ethos of all religion that cultures provide;

Religion is man-made, before it comes civilisation,
Power corrupts and in the God's name we divide a nation;

God loves us all, there is no discrimination,
Religions empower and induce separation.

God May Talk to You

We all conceive God in our own particular way,
How God manifests Himself, none can say;

Why have one Guru when He expresses Himself in myriad forms,
Communion with the Almighty defies all conventional norms;

The world is full of con artists, some are obvious,
Others may be law-abiding, but certainly dubious;

Saints experience that which only your eyes can tell,
In silence alone the secrets of existence dwell.

God Talks to Us

Disbelief puts our fate to blame,
God loves us all the same,
We are treated as we treat others,
It's tit for tat, and all in the game;

God talks to us in many ways,
Teaches us what a child says,
It's our conscience guiding us,
Through life's confusing maze;

When something untoward happens,
Luck is blamed and mood dampens,
It's a God-given opportunity, isn't it so?
Conflict sets in and thinking begins;

Thoughts deepen, the mind explores,
Light drowns the darkness galore,
This magic brings forth tears of joy,
In disguise heavenly blessings pour.

God wants a Win-Win

Rules, rituals and ethics are the doings of the authorities,
But desires, passions and morals are not their necessities;

In the name of religion, the deadliest wars are fought,
Rules are made for and by the smartest of the lot;

While the dedicated work with a passion,
The smart make money, the worthy get just a fraction;

Religion is not what we preach, but to surrender within,
God is omnipresent; let's enjoy and flourish with a win-win.

God-given Treasures

God has not forbidden anything; He has blessed us with life's pleasures,
Our guilt and insecurities have deprived us of the God-given treasures;

Why are women not blessed with the right companion?
To discover their heavenly selves through compassion;

Every woman is best characterised by her sweet spots,
They need someone to take pains to explore the lots;

A real man is a giver who fulfils the needs of the recipient by his actions,
Relishing the highest purity from the joy she demonstrates as a reaction.

Looking for Adventure

We are born to be wild, we keep looking for adventure,
Limiting ourselves to the rat race will be a misadventure;

Freedom means to live and let live,
To detach, forget and forgive;

If we do not adhere to the laws of nature, we are bound to regret,
With our thirst for power and possession, we shall remain under a threat;

Going against nature always has a price to pay,
It is tit for tat, nature gets back in a big way;

Corona is a fitting reply to the power-seekers who haven't spared even God,
For entrapping the aspirants of freedom, we have been caged with His nod;
The ones who surrender will have their blocks removed,
Those who don't budge will have their pleas disapproved;

How can we find a cure when all that's happening is unforeseen?
Building our immunity is in our hands, it's the God-given vaccine;

It works wonders, if you happen to come in contact with the diseased,
You get infected, your antibodies fight corona, your immunity is increased.

Grace of God

Enjoyment is not in being together but in yearning for it,
Like the two sides of a coin, to each other forever commit;

Memories are worth clinging to, not reality,
Attachment opposes love and has no similarity;

Getting rid of worldly attachment calls for soul-searching,
Loving yourself in the God within, the grace is far reaching.

Health is Godly

Being healthy is the God's way, that's what every spiritual path says,
If we work on our health, all our work becomes child's play;

Health strengthens us physically, mentally, emotionally,
Let go of attachments and love ourselves devotionally;

Attachment to the self is ego, loving yourself is loving God,
If we look after ourselves, we are bound to get His nod;

Health is proof of a strong character, the rest is subjective,
Fitness can be measured, that should be our only objective;

We listen to everyone but ourselves and go through hardship,
Knowing that love is God, health is religion and work is worship.

His Sole Control

When worried of completing a task, you don't,
You would succeed, but with doubt, you won't;

Our mind must be strong, neither hesitant, nor weak,
Lack of confidence will make our prospects bleak;

There are some who have no faith in themselves,
Others are enslaved by dogma, and blind faith delves;

The mind is ours, but we cannot tap or scroll it,
Because we are dependent on those who control it;

We are the creations of the God and in His sole control,
Why do we not surrender, for He resides in our soul!

Love is You

On a walk I came across someone who gave me a look,
Turning my face as we crossed, a glance I took,

All this happened with God's will, without purpose,
Then we had our part to play, and so became anxious,

Attraction brings attachment, not by the will of God,
This is not love; only a means to strive for His nod,

Love is you, independent of the one you love,
The purity within, when you are without a purpose,

True love is causeless, it's automatically one-sided,
Find love in all, this path of love is well-guided.

God and You

Ego is the only divide between others and you,
It's an inborn defect between the you and you;

You are born to clean up your misdeeds,
A God-given opportunity to achieve indeed;

One of you is carefree, knows not right from wrong,
The other one is righteous and bloody headstrong;

One of you is an unacceptable fool and a nobody,
The other one is enslaved to the norms and a somebody;

When you remove the divide between others and you,
There will be no divide between God and you.

Surrogate God

God in us sounds farfetched, so we follow a surrogate,
Whereas the devil in us goes by his mighty advocate;

We have just one weapon to show us the way,
It's love, the feeling within which God stays;

When you look for God within you,
You'll find Him within everyone too;

You will learn to love the way they are,
The truest version of themselves, by far;

Finding oneself appreciated by one's own essence,
Is like your soul achieving glory in your presence.

Faith in Self

Our relationship is with none but Him,
Whose cup of love is filled to the brim;

Why search when God resides within us?
He's yours, mine and ours, why discuss?

We debate issues and opinions are sought,
Religious lines are drawn, and wars are fought;

Killing in God's name comes from disbelief,
Only faith in oneself will bring us relief.

What does God want?

What God wants, none but God knows,
What we need, our minds never disclose,
Our needs may be far from our wants,
What our needs are, God alone knows;

We think that we know what we should,
Trying to compete is living in a falsehood,
We strive and pray for wealth and fame,
Not realising, all He does is for our good;

If He gives everything, we'll want more,
Our body and mind will be enslaved and sore,
With the slightest upheavals we'll collapse,
Those used to discomforts will thrive galore.

God-given Vaccine

Keep your mind at rest and the body in motion,
The other way round will hinder blood circulation;

Being glued to the television with a look of anguish,
Stresses you to become a couch potato in languish;

Do not allow negativity to come in the way of progress,
Ruining your health, mind and body to regress;

Wholehearted enjoyment is free, take in all you may glean
That's the way to build your immunity, with a God-given vaccine.

Religion is Not God

When God is love, and love is God
We love you all, we praise the Lord.

When God loves us, as we are His creativity
What are the killings in the name of Almighty?

Culture precedes all religions and thus
Religion is not made by God but by us.

Beliefs are so many, and they differ with every religion
But is religion God? Not at all, He is one and the only one!

God is omnipotent, being in everything and everyone,
Thereby He is in our beliefs, our fates and our religion.

What More You Want

What more you want, when He has given everything?
There is so much to enjoy, you'll not need anything!
When you throw out your inhibitions, you'll accept all He's given,
You'll realise that you've missed out on relishing something.

Truth cannot be spoken, as it is with a purpose,
Truth just spills out, when you're not cautious.
Truth dwells within, but doesn't surface
Truth is God, but He has no face.

Enjoyment through hardships is the redemption,
Ignorance of pain is the perfect justification.
Develop sweet spots of pain that are physical and emotional,
Creating all that is painful is a place of salvation.

Humanity and Religion

Humanity made progress with civilisation,
Invented numerous means of communication,
Culture and heritage are a source of talent,
To invoke their passions, and find occupation.

But religions showed up with insecurities and wars,
To uproot the civilised and their livelihood jarred,
Making them change their faith and creed,
Making converts and their theology barred.

Religions are in the custody of the godmen,
For having power over women and men,
Heaven and hell are where you are, all in the mind.
Humanity is dead, we're like animals in a den,
Religion feeds discipline, the rest will put you in a bind.

God is With You

Where do we need to go?
There is nothing to know

Where, why, how, and when,
All that we ask is irrelevant.

What is the burning question?
It is 'what', as we rightly mention.

Not what we think that does nothing,
The answer lies in doing something.

What we love to do is all in the mind,
What God wants for us is not behind.

All miseries are due to distrust,
Self-confidence is God's trust.
Do what you love and love what you do,
When you love yourself, God is with you.

Stop Bickering

When valuables cease to be important, values do,
When you walk with nature, the world comes to you.
Faltering, when He tests you, begin to realise and stop bickering.
And when you believe in Him, He smiles at you too.

The chaos is not in nature, but in trying to overcome it,
Engineers who sourced free energy have also learned to transmit.
Harmful gases, not renewables, are produced more by the rich,
It's time for the greedy, who blame the needy to quit.

Why do we feel that He expects too much from us?
Because we underestimate ourselves and have no trust.
Be prepared to accept anything that is least expected,
To change all the surprises to opportunities without a fuss.

Give and Take

Give and take is a social norm
The root cause of all the harm,
It should be confined to a transaction
Not friendship for it to remain warm;

Good people will keep doing good turns
Without expectations and without returns,
But for the purpose of goodwill being served
They thrive on satisfying others in return;

Where is all this boon from, are you aware?
No, I don't, it came from God knows where!
Transactions are only with God, let's have faith
You get what's best for you, if you don't compare.

Humanity and Religion

Humanity made progress with civilisation,
Invented numerous means of communication,
Culture and heritage are a source of talent,
To invoke their passions, and find occupation.

But religions showed up with insecurities and wars,
To uproot the civilised and their livelihood jarred,
Making them change their faith and creed,
Making converts and their theology barred.

Religions are in the custody of the godmen,
For having power over women and men,
Heaven and hell are where you are, all in the mind.
Humanity is dead, we're like animals in a den,
Religion feeds discipline, the rest will put you in a bind.

Where do we need to go

Where do we need to go?
There is nothing to know

Where, why, how, and when,
All that we ask is irrelevant.

What is the burning question?
It is 'what', as we rightly mention.

Not what we think that does nothing,
The answer lies in doing something.

What we love to do is all in the mind,
What God wants for us is not behind.

All miseries are due to distrust,
Self-confidence is God's trust.
Do what you love and love what you do,
When you love yourself, God is with you.

8. Reflections on Life

Blessings

Blessings from anyone are, in fact, blessings from God.
When your intention is right, you have His blessings, so long as you acknowledge and benefit from it.

Coincidences

There are no coincidences. It is His way of sending you a message.

Creation

If money is all we think of, we have no clue about God's creation.
God cannot bless you, His creations can.
My Lord tells me to live and let live, and to do no harm to myself or any of His creations.
If you fail to realise God, venerate all His creation, including yourself.

The Devil

We do not see God in others because it is easier to see the Devil in them.
The Devil in us has created God to justify our actions.
If you are God-fearing, it is the devil who you actually fear.

Divinity

If God is in each one of us, why don't we accept the divinity in the people around us?
When you reach the divinity within, you will reach it in others too.

Ego

The ego comes from worldly influence. Spirituality knows this and rises above.
Being attached to oneself is ego. Loving oneself is loving God.
Lord Shiva is purposeless and pure while Bajrangbali represents purpose and discipline. One is the positive energy and the other is the purpose behind it. They are two-in-ones like the ego and alter ego within us.

Faith

If we say that God is all-encompassing, we must have faith in His presence in each one of us.
There can be many beliefs but faith is singular.
A person who has faith in his fate is not an atheist.
Faith is when we go to our inner self where God dwells.

Fear and Worry

The moment you fear God, He is not God.
God is your friend. Why would you fear a friend?

Is God an outsider? If not, what is the worry? If yes, why worry?

Finding God

There is only one true way to connect to God. Your own.
God is willing to meet you halfway. Just walk the other half.
Why not just go with His plan?
God is beyond perception but we all perceive God in our own way, based on our individual beliefs and experiences. God is not one; there are as many Gods as people.
The more you listen, the more you realise that He has in fact been talking to you all the time.
There is nothing in this universe but God. Do not break your head looking for Him.

God is everywhere for us to behold if we seek Him within.
The location is known and the travel time is zero. Nonetheless, we fail to reach God.

Godmen

God is but the creation of godmen.
What is history but the power struggle between rulers and godmen?
Since time immemorial, it has always been a battle between God and godmen. Between truth and the alternate truth.
How would the godmen make money without religion?
Unlike a godman, a man of God does not seek disciples.
God enters our lives the moment we evict the godman from it.

God Speaks to Us

The more you listen, the more He speaks to you, directly through conversations you have with others, to subtler ways such as incidents. He is omnipresent!
God often speaks to us, but most of the time, we do not listen.

The Heart

Going towards the heart is akin to going towards God.
The fastest route to God is through the heart.

Life

God does everything for us but with twists and turns. Life is a script!
Life is bliss if you can put the monkey on His back because you know that He will gladly take it.

Losing the Way

How do we expect to reach God by bribing him or beating drums in the middle of the night?

How can anyone be free of corruption in this country, when extortion is done in the name of God?

God created man. Man corrupted God.

All the battles have been fought only to impose your perception of God on others, though God is too private to be shared.

We spend all our lives in search of a mirage. We want to be what we are not without realising the value of what we are. We go looking for God, not realising that Godliness is within us.

God wanted only one relationship between Him and us, but we have complicated that too.

You do not need loudspeakers to draw His attention. The moment you think right; you will feel his presence.

If we just understand what God has given us, we will have no time to see what he has given to others. Unfortunately, we do it the other way around.

We are believers in God but do not believe in Him.

'Is God with me?' is not the question. The question is, 'Am I with God?'

God is one of us, but we often exclude Him from our company.

You deprive yourself of His gifts despite Him having given you all that you need.

Love

If love is not an illusion, God is.
If you do not find love in God, look for God in your love.
True self-denial is always for the sake of love. If the love is for yourself, you are at one with God.
You really love God if you take Him for granted.
You will find the love of God in whoever lowers their guard.

The Mind

Let God make up my mind; I do not even know what I want!
The God of the mind needs agents. The God of the heart needs none.
Samadhi is the union between the heart and the mind as the body is left behind.
The only way to please God is to be in a state of mind to please others.

Morals and Ethics

We deny ourselves by judging things to be good or bad, moral or immoral, pure or impure.
Morals and ethics always go hand in hand as one without the other will go out of hand.

Receiving

He is all for you and will do everything for you but He wants you to earn it.

There are times when you feel that God is not fair to you. But in all fairness, the logic He applies is beyond your comprehension.

God may do things that are against our wishes but these certainly are not against our interests.

You will appreciate God's benevolence the day you realise that He provides what you need, not what you want.

Why do we feel that He expects too much from us, is it because we underestimate ourselves?

Religion

God did not make religion but religion invented God.

The theology of many cultures and religions is in harmony, and yet the differences are created by opportunists.

Before religion, there was no question of imposing our beliefs on others.

Peace and tranquillity may emerge if we ferry ourselves beyond religion.

History is full of battles in the name of God to impose a religion on others as a justification for the cause.

Hinduism is more a way of life than religion, so it is not imposed, and there are no converts.

Humanity made progress with civilisation, but religions arrived with insecurities and wars.

Every religion has to do with humanity, but we seek differences and become inhuman in the process.

Salvation

To see God in others is meditation. And to serve others is salvation.

Accepting penance is salvation while rejoicing in it is moksha.

The Scriptures

There is a lot to steal from the scriptures of the Almighty without being accused of plagiarism.

Repeated reading of religious scriptures is not prayer, absorbing them is.

Sin

Most of the sins are committed in the name of God. Buying and selling of favours in the name of God is a remunerative business.

Somebody and Nobody

Somebody up there keeps smiling at our goof-ups. If you do not let Him smile, He will raise the bar. Which is all the better!
We portray God as a Somebody, when, in fact, He is no slave to an identity, hence a Nobody.
Only when you are with Nobody, are you with God.

The Soul

A free soul is your body's caretaker and the source of the highest form of energy.
You liberate your soul when you surrender.
Wherever you see God, you see a soulmate. You can see God only when you see Him within you.
An unintended smile that appears on our lips is through our beaming eyes, the windows to our souls. It is a spiritual encounter.
There is a lot to imbibe from religious places and ceremonies as the atmosphere is serene; everyone is distanced from the rat race and is closer to their soul.

Spiritualism

Spirituality is linked to the logic of the Beyond.

A true man of God is one who keeps himself physically, mentally, emotionally and spiritually healthy.

Shri Ganesha – the Lord of creativity and balance – is the Master of prosperity on the one hand and the Master of spirituality on the other.

Spiritual energy will satisfy needs and overcome greed.

The Third Eye

The third eye, also known as the inner eye of wisdom, is the one that balances the other two. It is straight and direct; the other two are at an angle and report to either side of the brain. The right eye looks for purity and positivity while the left eye, for purpose and discipline. They are controlled by the third eye, which is in the centre of Lord Shiva's forehead.

Beyond our vision is the fourth dimension which can only be seen with Shiva's third eye. You must balance the left and the right eye to get there. This can only be done with an empty mind.

Trust

The day you trust yourself, you will trust God.

God does not care if you are not trustworthy, He wants you to be just trusting.

We do not believe in destiny because we don't trust God.

He tells us what to do, corrects us from time to time, pats us on our back when we do things right and shows us glimpses of the brightest things to happen. Yet we fail to trust Him!

Truth

By running away from ourselves, we are running away from truth, purity and God.

Mankind resorts to the alternate truth because the actual truth is beyond it.

When you embrace the bitter truth, you embrace God.

www.ingramcontent.com/pod-product-compliance
Lightning Source LLC
LaVergne TN
LVHW061345080526
838199LV00094B/7363